200 Tips
for Gardening
in the Shade

❧ ❧

200 Tips
for Gardening
in the Shade

Pam Wolfe

CHICAGO
REVIEW
PRESS

Library of Congress Cataloging-in-Publication Data

Wolfe, Pamela.

200 tips for gardening in the shade / Pamela Wolfe.—1st ed.

p. cm.

ISBN 1-55652-369-6

1. Shade-tolerant plants. 2. Gardening in the shade. I. Title: Two hundred tips for gardening in the shade. II. Title.

SB434.7 .W66 2000

635.9'543—dc21   99-047691

CIP

Cover and interior design: Hendrickson Creative Communications

Published by Chicago Review Press, Incorporated

814 North Franklin Street

Chicago, Illinois 60610

ISBN 1-55652-369-6

Printed in the United States of America

5 4 3 2 1

*To Robin—growing for the shade,
and Candy—gardening in the shade.*

Contents

✌: ✌:

✌:

Introduction

Nearly every gardener contends with the challenges of shade. At every talk or interview I give, I hear comments such as "I can't have a garden; I have too much shade" or "What can I grow in the shade besides hosta and impatiens?" If peonies, roses, and daylilies once bloomed beneath trees that have now grown tall and full, the changes needed to develop a dazzling shade garden remain elusive for many gardeners. Instead, frustration grows, and the garden is gradually abandoned to the ground cover of least resistance.

Virtually every home has some shade. Every building has a north side, an overhang. Nearly every homeowner has at least one tree. As a sapling matures, the garden evolves. The shade sought after on a scorching summer afternoon brings with it the need for a whole new garden. The change is so slow that many wonder why plants that once bloomed vigorously have stopped; why gardens that once flourished are in decline. Every gardener finds that plants that once stood straight and full have turned floppy and spindly over time. The reason is the growing shade.

Flowers in the sun attract attention. Many new gardeners are captivated by the colorful, showy, glitzy look and the lush spectrum of color and form. In shade these hopes for a brilliant mosaic fade quickly, and the enthusiasm for building a garden wanes. A spectacular shade garden takes an attention to detail overlooked and unneeded in the flamboyance of a sunny border. Color in the shade is subtle but no less interesting. Flowers still bloom. Texture and form still create a rhythm of beauty. An intricately developed shade garden has many layers that intensify the serenity of the landscape and satisfy the eye and soul.

Degrees
of Shade

❧ ❧

 Shade is one of the most elusive and indefinite terms in gardening. When a plant is in the sun, it is obvious. But how many hours of direct light make a spot "sunny" or "shady"? Except in the most open sites or in treeless, newly built subdivisions, light hitting an entire garden from dawn to dusk is rather rare. The challenge is to evaluate whether an area has light shade, part shade, full shade, or very dense shade. Learning to read the landscape is an ongoing task of all gardeners.

If plants grow much taller than expected and defy staking, they are likely in too much shade. Many gardeners realize they have a shady garden only when plants that should grow 18 inches tall tower to two or three feet and then fall over. When a plant receives too little light, it gets "leggy" and weak. Some gardeners may think the plant is getting too much fertilizer. However, tallness and weakness are not symptoms of overfertilizing. They are the first telltale signs of too much shade.

Gardening in Light Shade

Light shade, shielding the sun for only an hour or two each day, provides many flowering plants with a respite from the intensity of summer's heat and light. Throughout the central and southern states, midsummer sun causes flowers to fade quickly. Many shade-loving plants like impatiens and *Ligularia* spp. wilt during the heat of the day, only to perk up as soon as the shade is cooler. Roses, lilies, and nasturtiums also suffer from midsummer heat. Some light afternoon shade shelters them from the intense summer glare and helps the flowers hold their color. Celandine poppy *(Stylophorum diphyllum)* goes dormant during midsummer in southern states where the heat is most intense.

Flowering plants that thrive in cool climates generally benefit from the protection of light shade. Trees help to cool the garden even when they stand at some distance from these delicate plants. Their long shadows stretching across the garden at three o'clock in the afternoon bring relief to hot, dry midsummer landscapes.

 Trees whose lowest branches start 20 to 30 feet from the ground create much less shade than trees with limbs hanging low. A tree with an upright growth habit tends to give less shade than a widely stretching tree. The trunk alone really doesn't create much shade. If the branches begin high off the ground, even a tree with large leaves and a dense canopy, like an oak, produces only light shade.

 The small, fine-textured leaves of thornless honey locust (*Gleditsia triacanthos*) filter light like a lace curtain, barely casting a shadow. These and other trees with a similar open form and small leaves have gained popularity in part because lawns grow easily under them. Although carrying larger leaves, green ash (*Fraxinus pennsylvanica*) allows sun-loving flowering plants like coneflowers, sedum, and roses to grow beneath. Trees that reduce heat and glare while producing light shade give a wide range of growing options.

 In light shade, the graceful, tubular, slightly pendulous blooms of flowering tobacco (*Nicotiana* spp.) redefine what flowering annuals can bring to the garden. Annuals tend to grow in a blanket of color. Petunias, marigolds, and even impatiens paint the ground with electric effect. In contrast, flowering tobacco stands at least 18 inches to three feet tall. Its deep red, rose, pink to white, and pale green flowers add texture and form as well as color to the garden. Particularly attractive, with long, lime-green tubes dangling from the top of three-foot plants, is *N. langsdorfii*.

The Partly Shady Garden

 The difference between light shade and part shade is not exact. Various factors affect how much light is actually striking the garden. The total amount of light a plant gets is a combination of the duration of the light and its intensity. If the light is less intense when it strikes the plant, it should shine for more hours. If the light is more intense, less time is required to give the same total amount to the plant. At noon the angle of the sun is more direct than earlier or later in the day. This results in the most intense light.

When trees or buildings are at some distance from the garden, the shade they produce is often difficult to recognize. Shadows cast until late morning and again by midafternoon create part shade. The earlier in the afternoon that shadows reach a bed or the later a bed remains in shadow in the morning, the more shady the garden. Less than six hours of light during the middle of the day creates a condition of reduced light for most plants, and they may begin to bloom less and grow taller than expected.

Although most flowering shrubs won't bloom in heavy shade, they tolerate part shade, and some shelter protects their buds from heavy late-winter frost. Plant early-blooming shrubs and trees with an evergreen on their southwest side. The flowers will emerge more slowly and there will be less likelihood that the blossoms will turn to brown slime. When spring-flowering bulbs are lightly sheltered from prevailing winds and full sun, their flowers last longer than those blooming in very exposed sites.

In harsher climates, trees of any kind provide some protection against early autumn and late spring frosts for tender or early-blooming plants. Sudden cold snaps damage woody plants such as forsythia and magnolia, as well as many spring-flowering bulbs. A web of branches creates a netlike barrier above the garden that slows the flow of air as it rises and falls and mediates rapid changes in temperature, helping to ensure consistent bloom in the garden.

 Although deciduous trees provide shade during the summer, they allow winter and early spring light to filter through their leafless branches. Similarly, deciduous conifers used as a screen or hedge create privacy in the summer garden and admit light across the winter horizon. Dawn redwood *(Metasequoia glyptostroboides),* bald cypress *(Taxodium distichum),* and larch *(Larix* spp.) drop their needles every fall. Grown on the south and west exposures, these deciduous conifers bring the benefits of passive solar heating and cooling to the landscape and to the home.

Working with Heavy Shade

Under deciduous trees that produce heavy shade in midsummer, the best color comes before the trees leaf out. While light still pours onto the forest floor, most spring flowers bloom. Some that make a colorful display are Virginia bluebell *(Mertensia virginica)*, bloodroot *(Sanguinaria canadensis)*, Dutchman's-breeches *(Dicentra cucullaria)*, and trout lily *(Erythronium* spp.). As the season continues, leaves mature, and shade deepens, the foliage of these early spring beauties becomes dormant. All traces of them vanish until next spring. They fall into a class of woodland plants known as spring ephemerals.

Although daffodils bloom in woodland glades, they need exposure to sun in the spring. The more impenetrable the shade, the less they bloom. Planting near or under deciduous trees that leaf out slowly is ideal. Avoid planting them under or even near evergreens or deciduous trees with very early or dense shade, like most maples. Situated in the right spot, daffodils bloom year after year. As the trees grow and produce more and more shade, the plants flower less.

White and pastel narcissus tolerate lower light than the yellow trumpet daffodils. Since bleaching of red tones occurs in strong light, narcissus in pastel shades with a tinge of orange or red actually benefit from light shade. The eye-catching beauty of these bicolors stands out in the muted light of the spring shade garden. Bicolors planted in combination with pale blue pansies, forget-me-nots, or grape hyacinths are striking. White narcissus blend with a wide range of colors but look particularly spectacular with primroses.

 Although all bulbs stop flowering if they become too crowded, usually narcissus won't need to be transplanted for many years. However, when they are grown in too much shade, they will also stop blooming. Wait until their foliage dies back, and transplant them in June or July. Dig, then divide the bulbs and transplant them to a sunnier area of the garden. Since the newly divided bulbs are small, they may need a couple of years to start flowering again.

 Not all trees are equal in a shade garden. Norway maples combine large leaves and a dense canopy with a shallow, thick root system. These maples efficiently suck water out of the ground, robbing moisture from any undergrowth trying to coexist. Growing anything under them is one of a gardener's biggest challenges. Only after coaxing with regular watering will a few of the most shade-tolerant plants take hold. To slow water loss further, mulch around newly planted ground cover. By the time the maple's roots grow into the mulch, the ground cover should be well established.

 Conifers, or cone-bearing trees, produce the densest shade of all. Beneath a forest of pines, spruces, firs, and cedars, very little grows. For this very dark and often dry site, choose plants that grow very little in a season. Japanese spurge *(Pachysandra terminalis)*, English ivy *(Hedera helix)*, and periwinkle or myrtle *(Vinca minor)* are ground covers that will grow near the drip line, or direct shade, of these trees.

 Eager to add light, many gardeners trim up the lower limbs of conifers like spruce and fir. Pruning up evergreen branches almost always fails to improve their appearance. When sweeping lower limbs are pruned high off the ground, trees lose their natural beauty and relatively little light is gained. Try to limit the amount of pruning in favor of drip-line plantings of slow-growing, shade- and drought-tolerant plants.

Japanese spurge *(Pachysandra terminalis),* **bigleaf wintercreeper** *(Euonymus fortunei),* **and Canada wild ginger** *(Asarum canadense)* **grow in fairly dense coniferous shade.** Although wintercreeper and wild ginger produce inconspicuous flowers, Japanese spurge produces a lovely spring display of tiny white flowers in mild climates or when it is protected by a winter layer of snow. In the spring, near the edge of shade cast by conifers, columbine *(Aquilegia canadensis),* foam flower *(Tiarella cordifolia,* and Jacob's ladder *(Polemonium* spp.) produce showy flowers. In the fall, beds of hardy cyclamen *(Cyclamen hederifolium)* add colorful blossoms.

The dark pockets and alleys produced by groups of evergreens or under wide overhangs along the north sides of buildings are often carpeted with nothing but a blanket of needles. These spots are ideal for recreating the natural floor of a boreal forest. Bunchberry *(Cornus canadensis),* with whorls of four leaves topped by delicate white flowers in the spring and eye-catching red berries in the fall, or the smooth elliptical leaves of Canada mayflower *(Maianthemum canadense)* carpet the woodlands with color and texture.

As under Norway maples, the challenge under a deep three- to four-foot north-facing overhang comes from the dry soil as much as from the heavy shade. Start planting at the edge of the overhang. Here rain will water the young roots of new plantings. Pachysandra, English ivy, and *Vinca minor* will slowly creep toward the house. Hosta leaves arch in a fountain of growth. With their roots planted near the edge, their foliage reaches back into the shady dry spots under the overhang.

 The serene setting of a climax beech-maple forest consists of towering giants as widely spaced as pillars in a cathedral. The shade is so dense that seedlings of most other trees cannot easily grow. This is called a climax forest because its plant communities are stable. Other species do not replace these mature trees. The natural process that results in a climax community takes over a hundred years. Re-creating one in the landscape takes planning, weeding, watering, and time.

 For the shadiest gardens, build on the simplicity of nature. Allow wildflowers to reseed themselves. Their spontaneous flow determines the shape of the most naturalistic garden. Overplanting and artificial grouping results in a busy, unsettled effect. Keep the planting simple. In the spring, masses of Virginia bluebell *(Mertensia virginica),* rue anemone *(Anemonella thalictroides),* trillium *(Trillium* spp.), mayapple *(Podophyllum peltatum),* and bloodroot *(Sanguinaria canadensis)* jockey for position. During the summer, the persistent foliage of Solomon's seal *(Polygonatum* spp.), jack-in-the-pulpit *(Arisaema* spp.), ferns, woodland sedges *(Carex* spp.), columbine, foam flower, Jacob's ladder, and hardy cyclamen maintain the garden's design.

 In an open woodland, spring wildflowers such as trillium, lady's slipper *(Cypripedium* spp.), rue anemone, false rue anemone *(Isopyrum biternatum),* bloodroot, and Dutchman's-breeches cover the forest floor in the spring. Most of midsummer finds very little growing on the forest floor. The cool, open shade of the woods reverberates with simplicity. No adornments enhance the play of light and shadow. By late fall, the quiet retreat is carpeted with yellow leaves while the brilliant fall light shines through the roof of yellow still left on the trees.

Seasons in
the Shade

❧ ❧

Spring in the Shade

A carpet of white wildflowers completes the rhythm of the spring shade garden. In the spring, native wildflowers such as rue anemone *(Anomella thalictroides)*, false rue anemone *(Isopyrum biternatum)*, bloodroot *(Sanguinaria canadensis)*, squirrel corn *(Dicentra canadensis)*, and Dutchman's-breeches *(D. cucullaria)* form a delicate white mosaic on the forest floor. Standing slightly taller, shooting star *(Dodecatheon meadia)* delicately shines in the Midwest prairie soils, while giant white trillium *(Trillium grandiflorum)* spectacularly radiates and thrives in well-drained sites. Even a small planting of

❧

these ephemeral white flowers appears as lace spread over the ground.

 Popular white-flowering ground covers include *Lamium* **spp., sweet woodruff** *(Galium odoratum)*, **and lily-of-the-valley** *(Convallaria majalis)*. *Vinca minor*—myrtle—produces one of the best blue blossoms for the shade garden. A very beautiful cultivar, *V. minor* 'Jekyll's White', has tiny dark green shiny leaves highlighted by pure white flowers. In slightly acid soils, foam flower *(Tiarella cordifolia)* forms drifts of white candle-like clusters of blossoms in early summer. With the white-flowering trees and shrubs, these ground covers complete a rhythm of light that echoes through the shade garden.

 The white bell-like flowers of *Leucojum* **spp. bloom in the early spring before the trees block out the sun.** These delicate white spring-flowering bulbs are underused. Their small, drooping blossoms dangle in a line along the one- to three-foot flowering stalks. Their narrow leaves resemble those of daffodils, and like daffodils, the leaves disappear shortly after flowering. When planted among sweeps of *Vinca minor,* Allegheny spurge *(Pachysandra procumbens),* or bigleaf wintercreeper *(Euonymus fortunei),* they add surprising beauty to the spring garden. Their only requirements are well-drained soil and some early spring sun.

 Snowdrops (*Galanthus* spp.) bloom in late winter or the earliest days of spring. When planted in a sheltered spot, winter is not too early to see their tiny bell-like flowers. Planted with an evergreen ground cover like pachysandra or vinca, they earn their name. In regions of the country where winter and spring linger interchangeably, snowdrops may last for several weeks. Easier to grow than other winter bloomers, such as Christmas and Lenten rose (*Helleborus* spp.), *Galanthus* still does not spread with abandon, as do those other harbingers of spring, glory-of-the-snow *(Chionodoxa luciliae)* or squill *(Scilla sibirica)*.

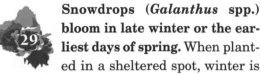 **By late spring, when the stands of elderberries bloom, the weeks of spring flowering come to a climax.** White-flowering trees such as Japanese styrax *(Styrax japonica)*, Carolina silverbell *(Halesia carolina)*, and hawthorn (*Crataegus* spp.) add to the overall brilliance of the season. Even shrubs that don't tend to form natural masses have exquisite flowers for the spring shade garden. *Fothergilla gardenii* and *F. major* flower with small white puffs that fill the air with

a delightful fragrance. Small white flowers may seem puny, but en masse and over a long season they give visual energy and sparkle to the garden.

 Late spring—and early summer—flowering perennials include lady's mantle *(Alchemilla mollis)* and masterwort *(Astrantia major)*. Both bloom with small clusters of flowers that produce a stunning effect. Astrantia's small starlike flowers of pink and green form umbrella-shaped clusters. *Alchemilla*'s small yellow flowers grow in large, airy clusters that float like clouds above their soft yellow-green leaves. Although both plants have small flowers, their mass effect is substantial. Since many spring wildflowers finish flowering in the very early spring, these two plants keep the garden in bloom later in the season.

 Late spring to midsummer native American wildflowers add variety of form and texture to the garden for the entire season. Some of the most notable include goat's beard *(Aruncus dioicus)*, golden ragwort *(Senecio aureus)*, blue-eyed grass *(Sisyrinchium* spp.), speckled wood lily *(Clintonia umbellulata)*, false Solomon's seal *(Smilacina racemosa)*, and false goat's beard *(Astilbe biternata)*. The golden ragwort, false

Solomon's seal, and goat's beard grow in rich, calcareous, wet woods and thickets. The various species of blue-eyed grass grow from damp, sandy shores to dry, open prairies.

The native flowering plants celandine poppy or wood poppy *(Stylophorum diphyllum)*, native dwarf tickseed *(Coreopsis auriculata)*, and wild bleeding heart *(Dicentra eximia)* give their showiest flowering display in the spring and continue to flower throughout the growing season. The bright yellow celandine poppy spreads easily and naturally from seed. Its color radiates through the shadows of a woodland glade. The delicate pink flowers of wild bleeding heart grow as a short bouquet from the center of its cluster of lacy leaves. With only three to four hours of sun a day, dwarf tickseed flowers first in the spring and then with scattered flowers throughout the season.

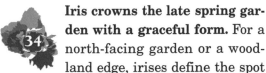

Iris crowns the late spring garden with a graceful form. For a north-facing garden or a woodland edge, irises define the spot where they are planted. In light shade, the tall, delicate Siberian iris (*Iris sibirica*) and the short, robust Japanese roof iris (*Iris tectorum*) thrive. Although each flower lasts only one day, the blooms hold their color and fresh look longer when shaded from the heat of the midday sun, and the cool shade keeps them coming more slowly.

 One of the most enchanting flowers for shade, primrose (*Primula* spp.) brings images of fairy tales, long, flowing dresses, and tea parties on the lawn. Grown in moist but well-drained shade, they flower in bright nosegays that range from yellow, red, and rose to blue and deep purple. Several species produce the same eye-catching effect. The easiest to grow is the yellow *Primula vulgaris*. Cultivars of *Primula japonica* also grow widely in American gardens. The delicate pink candelabra or drumstick primrose is limited to zones six and seven. Given deep organic soil that drains efficiently, the plants emerge early in the spring and look great with the small, shiny, dark green leaves and small white flowers of *Vinca minor* 'Jekyll's White'.

 In woodlands or shady spots with damp soil, two different plants commonly called forget-me-not thrive. In early spring, *Myosotis* spp. blooms as a low-growing carpet of tiny blue flowers. If the soil is dry, the plants may die after the flowers form seedpods. Otherwise they persist throughout the season and flower again the following season. Even if the plants die, they spread easily by seed. *Brunnera macrophylla* grows slightly taller, spreads more slowly, and withstands slightly drier soils. The plants have broadly heart-shaped leaves and stand eight to 12 inches tall. After the flowers fade, they blend well with a variety of other shade plants such as geraniums, ferns, and lungwort (*Pulmonaria* spp.).

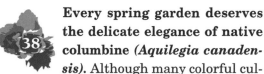

Tree peonies *(Paeonia suffruticosa)* are outstanding spring-flowering plants for light shade. As trees grow and shade increases, most late spring–flowering plants, including herbaceous peonies, quit flowering. But tree peonies need shade from intense sun—otherwise color is leached from their blooms and their flowers fade quickly.

Although herbaceous peonies die back to the ground each fall, tree peonies are a small to medium woody shrub that does not die back. The satiny smooth petals of their large single or double flowers look like silk. When they bloom, they are a focal point. After flowering, the large, deep green foliage adds form and texture to the garden.

Every spring garden deserves the delicate elegance of native columbine *(Aquilegia canadensis)*. Although many colorful cultivars of columbine tempt the garden palette, the straight species outperforms them all.

The pale orange and yellow bicolored flowers tolerate more shade and resist more insects and diseases than the brighter yellows, pinks, and blues of the developed cultivars. All columbines require slightly acid, well-drained, moist soil. In the right spot they flower for three to four weeks and hold their foliage for the rest of the summer.

Summer in the Shade

Summer-flowering shrubs enhance and lighten the garden. During midsummer, white ball-like clusters bloom on smooth hydrangea *(Hydrangea arborescens)* and oak-leaf hydrangea *(H. quercifolia).* Their substantial clusters of small flowers last long after the fresh, white glow fades from their petals. Beige dried flower heads remain on the bush until clipped off. Another summer beauty, Carolina summersweet *(Clethra alnifolia),* adds a strong, delightful fragrance as well as delicate candles of small flowers with a loose, open form. Although it is usually white, a striking light red form, 'Ruby Skies', adds color, scent, and light to the garden.

Often considered the mainstay of the summer shade garden, hostas are not all equal. The less green the foliage, the more sun the variety requires. Stunning newer cultivars such as 'White Christmas', 'Patriot',

'Fire and Ice', 'Loyalist', 'Masquerade', 'Medusa', 'Cherry Berry', 'Flame Stitch', and 'Fairmaiden' require filtered light or early morning direct sun to thrive. The larger and more pure the white portions of the leaf, the more light they need.

 Summer whites lighten summer shade. Two stately white summer-flowering plants are black snakeroot *(Cimicifuga racemosa)* and goat's beard *(Aruncus dioicus)*. They are ideal for low-lying, damp spots. Black snakeroot flowers on tall, thin candle-like stalks. The deeper the shade, the more likely the five- to eight-foot stalks will need staking. Goat's beard flowers on shorter plants with a more feathery look. They both blend well with royal, cinnamon, and ostrich fern as well as with spiderwort *(Tradescantia virginiana)*.

 In regions where summer heat is another word for steam, the wispy plumes of goat's beard and black snakeroot's white-flowering spikes may last a week or less. In the damp, cool shade of northern or northeastern gardens, they may flower for several weeks. Southern gardeners often use *Cimicifuga americana,* a shorter and more useful plant for hot summer gardens. After flowering, black snakeroot forms stunning red berries. Goat's beard's white flowers just turn brown. Both form bushy, arching stands of dissected leaves that are very attractive.

 Use tropical houseplants in the summer shade garden. The shadiest part of the garden takes on a lush tropical look with indoor plants. In an otherwise bare spot, plant a small group of African violets, a cluster of peperomias, some baby tears, and an artillery fern or two. When the soil is warm (at least 60°F), bury pots of houseplants in the ground. When evening temperatures drop to less than 55°F in the fall, take the pots out of the ground again.

 In midsummer, white flowers of bottlebrush buckeye (*Aesculus parviflora*), goat's beard, and bright yellow ligularia (*Ligularia dentata* 'Desdemona' or *L. stenocephala* 'The Rocket') produce spectacular flowers. Although the key to long-lasting displays is adequate moisture combined with the cooling effect of the shade, these plants do poorly in heavy clay soils that drain slowly. Since bottlebrush buckeye easily spreads out to cover an area nearly 15 feet wide, it may be too large for smaller gardens. Instead, use Carolina summersweet. Its pleasing fragrance makes it a superb shrub for any garden.

Ligularia 'The Rocket' blooms in early summer with yellow flowers well described by the name. The tall spikes of small blossoms rise above clumps of large, deeply toothed leaves. Moist, lightly shaded spots suit this eye-catching plant. With shorter pink candle-like flowers, the showy member of the knotweed family, *Polygonum bistorta* 'Superbum', blends well with 'The Rocket'. Although most knotweeds lack any redeeming ornamental quality, in the right spot, this plant fits the bill.

Tall ferns stand as a backdrop for ephemeral as well as persistent perennials. Ostrich fern *(Matteuccia pensylvanica)* gives a shade garden a feeling of prehistoric beauty. Typically, this fern stand three feet tall, but in very fertile and damp soils, where it spreads rapidly by rhizomes, it can reach five feet. The light yellow-green fronds grow as lush and thick as plumes on the birds from which it gets its name. Other tall ferns include cinnamon fern *(Osmunda cinnamomea),* named for its reddish brown spore-bearing fronds that stand like sticks of cinnamon in the winter garden, and royal fern *(Osmunda regalis).* Of the three common tall ferns, royal fern needs the wettest soil. Its distinctive fronds have a coarser, fanlike appearance.

Mid-sized ferns blend well with many shade garden plants. Ladyfern *(Athyrium filix-femina)* grows full, finely textured whorls of fronds that blend well with spiderwort *(Tradescantia virginiana),* Solomon's seal *(Polygonatum commutatum),* and shorter plants such as Canada wild ginger *(Asarum canadense)* and lungwort. Other common mid-sized ferns, Christmas fern *(Polystichum acrostichoides),* hay-scented fern *(Dennstaedtia punctilobula),* and crested shield fern *(Dryopteris cristata)* grow in the characteristic clumps that spread only slowly through the garden. These are excellent planted together in a mosaic of textures. Blending them together in irregular patches gives a resonant combination.

A popular plant for the shade, astilbe *(Astilbe)* comes in a wide range of sizes. The feathery plumes of the traditional standard form range between 12 and 24 inches tall. Newer cultivars top out at only eight inches. The distinctive plumes of the taller varieties blend well with lamium, English ivy, or other muted, low-growing plants. Shorter cultivars, including 'Sprite' and 'Pumila', work well as an edging to a walk or with the low-growing, tricolor carpet bugle (*Ajuga reptans* 'Burgundy Glow'). Their finely dissected leaves create an appealing textural blend long after their midsummer flowers fade.

White berries on shrubs accent the shadows of fall. As green fades into autumn yellows, reds, and brown, the small light-colored fruit of snowberry *(Symphoricarpos albus)* and Japanese beautyberry *(Callicarpa japonica)* create points of reflected light. Plant these shrubs in clusters or masses at the edge of the woodland garden. Even at a distance, small clusters of berries stand out. Against the mottled red leaves of oakleaf hydrangea and the clear yellow of spicebush *(Lindera benzoin),* small white berries add substance and texture to the fall garden.

Plants That Stretch Through the Seasons

Long-blooming shade perennials flower for weeks and even months. In mild climates, Christmas rose *(Helleborus* spp.) blooms in December. In colder regions, Lenten rose *(Helleborus* spp.) emerges in March and holds its flowers all season. The tiny yellow flowers of *Corydalis lutea* and delicate pink blooms of showy bleeding heart *(Dicentra eximia)* produce new flowers from late spring until fall. Although celandine poppy produces its fullest flushes of bright yellow flowers in late spring, in cooler climates it blooms sporadically all summer. The delicate fall flowers of purple toadflax *(Linaria purpurea)* last four to six weeks in autumn.

The arching stems of false Solomon's seal *(Smilacina racemosa)* end with a showy plume of tiny white flowers. The wide lilylike leaves flank the stem in uniform line. Like soldiers on parade, these plants seem to stand in formation with the stems and flowers all presented in one direction. Their leaves persist throughout the summer. By fall, where they once flashed white flowers, they carry blood-red berries. The yellowing leaves look battleworn from insects eating tiny holes in them. Where the seeds fall, new plants sprout, and false Solomon's seal moves slowly across the woodland.

Sedges (*Carex* spp.) are among the most notable grasslike plants for shade. Sedges often grow in clumps rather than as a solid, uniform turf. Ornamental sedges are not mowed; they grow with narrow, arching foliage similar to lilyturf or mondo grass. These two have wider leaves and are not as cold hardy as sedges. Cultivars of Japanese sedges *Carex morrowii* and *C. oshimensis* 'Evergold' are among the most colorful and widely used. Attractive native American sedges *C. jamesii, C. pensylvanica, C. plantaginea,* and *C. eburnea* grow well in many woodlands.

Design Ideas
for Shade

❦ ❦

The Woodland Garden

Yews (*Taxus* spp.) and hemlocks (*Tsuga canadensis*) tolerate more shade than other conifers and are a natural backdrop for the shade garden. Yews' dense foliage blocks undesirable views and forms a privacy screen. Their deep green color provides an excellent background for the delicate flowers of native spring ephemera. Hemlocks' smaller needles have a lighter texture, producing a similar yet a softer effect.

❦

Mass plantings enhance the effect of small-flowering wildflowers. Grouped together, even larger-flowered daffodils resonate. When naturalized in large drifts, the effect is a vista impossible to achieve any other way. As the plants spread by seed, the natural flow of the drift may change slightly from year to year. Although the tiny individual flowers disappear in the mass of bloom, the panorama pulls viewers inward toward the finer detail.

Observe natural places to see how the plants flow in large sweeps. Clusters of individual species flow around each other as if liquid. Groups of plants are not lined up in rows or even in circles. For a woodland garden to be a replica of the real thing, the flow must look natural and casual. Bed lines that curve tightly seem to wiggle. They look less natural than ones that curve gently, with a smooth, continuous line.

Although shade gardens have the reputation of being all foliage and no flowers, a sequence of flowering plants can give color to the shadowy parts of the landscape. In spring, combinations of pale blue amsonia, pink and white bleeding heart *(Dicentra spectabilis),* and a mat of blue flowers produced by forget-me-not or *Vinca minor* serve as a colorful beginning. Add to this the variety of spring bulbs for a kaleidoscope of color. For the summer garden, *Astilbe,* black snakeroot *(Cimicifuga racemosa), Ligularia, Tradescantia,* and the flowers of various hostas command attention. By fall, Japanese anemone, cardinal flower, woodland aster, and white snakeroot complete the progression of bloom.

 White-flowering trees and shrubs add light and create depth in the shade garden. In the spring, a succession of blooming viburnum (*Viburnum* spp.), dogwood (*Cornus* spp.), elderberry (*Sambucus* spp.), and chokecherry resembles white waves penetrating the growing shade. Tiny candles of flowers on groups of chokecherries and short white clusters of flowers on American plums signal the beginning. Soon the stems of gray dogwood arch to the ground at the edge of shade, covered with white flower heads. Next the viburnums bloom, with their flat clusters of pale flowers forming a veil of white over the emerging green of the woods.

 Woodland ephemera emerge, bloom, fade, and become dormant in a matter of weeks. Some delicate native spring ephemerals are shooting star *(Dodecatheon meadia),*

spring beauty *(Claytonia virginica)*, trout lily or dogtooth violet *(Erythronium* spp.), wild leek or ramp *(Allium tricoccum)*, Dutchman's-breeches *(Dicentra cucullaria)*, squirrel corn *(D. canadensis)*, bloodroot *(Sanguinaria canadensis)*, and wild hyacinth *(Camassia scilloides)*. Taller ephemera are mayapple *(Podophyllum peltatum)* and Virginia bluebell *(Mertensia virginica)*. Mayapple and Virginia bluebell grow up to two feet tall. When they die back to the ground, they leave a hole. Using them with the persistent foliage of Canada wild ginger *(Asarum canadense)*, wood fern *(Dryopteris dilatata)*, and ladyfern *(Athyrium filix-femina)* helps fill the space left when they go dormant.

A number of low-growing spring-flowering plants spread vigorously in shade gardens. A clear blue blanket of tiny squill *(Scilla sibirica)* grows easily and spreads by dropping seeds. The plants grow only four to six inches tall. In early spring they emerge, flower, and go dormant within a month. Squill blooms a few weeks after snowdrops *(Galanthus* spp.). Planted under the low-slung branches of magnolias, they look striking. Glory-of-the-snow *(Chionodoxa luciliae)* flowers with the same vigor, producing pale blue starlike flowers with white centers.

Hostas dominate many shade gardens. The variety of sizes, colors, and even textures makes them more versatile than almost any other plant. They bloom on long stems held high above mushroom-shaped mounds of leaves. Most have small, pale flowers that detract from their stunning foliage, but a few produce very beautiful, large, fragrant flowers. The white, five-inch-long trumpets of *Hosta plantaginea* 'Grandiflora' bloom in late summer with a delightful scent.

 Avoid planting a narrow ring of hosta around the trunk of a tree. A shade garden and hosta deserve better. Visually tie nearby trees together with a combination of shade plants in clusters rather than rows. Vary their height and texture. For seasonal color, intersperse plants that flower, like columbine *(Aquilegia canadensis),* bellwort *(Uvularia* spp.), bloodroot, and wild geranium *(Geranium maculatum).* Use the entire area under the drip line, or direct shade, of the tree.

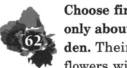 **Choose fine-textured plants for only about one-third of the garden.** Their delicate foliage and flowers will highlight and unify stronger-textured plants, but a garden of predominantly fine textures loses its sense

of rhythm. The majority of a garden's plants should have a medium to coarse texture. In the shade garden, hellebore, pachysandra, brunnera, wintercreeper, lungwort, and medium- to broadleaf hosta establish a framework and line. Accent them with fine-textured showy bleeding heart *(Dicentra eximia),* sedges *(Carex* spp.), narrow-leaf small hosta, ferns, and yellow corydalis *(Corydalis lutea).*

 Between stepping-stones or under a tree, mosses and liverworts are part of a natural woodland glade. In areas where moisture hangs in the air like a curtain, a moss and liverwort garden is beautiful and serene. Although the flat, scale-like liverwort needs an almost constant trickle of water, moss adapts to nearly any shady, humid spot. Water down stepping-stones in the morning and evening to encourage moss to come. As with any plant grown strictly for its foliage, many moss species grow with slightly different colors and textures.

Pathways and Edges

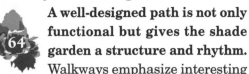

A well-designed path is not only functional but gives the shade garden a structure and rhythm. Walkways emphasize interesting features and provide a framework for plantings as well as bringing more flowers and textures into view. Have the walk pass near or around particularly attractive trees or shrubs. Walking close to large horizontal branches or through alleys of flowering plants intensifies the perception of garden.

A walkway need not lead anywhere. As a path winds out of view, it creates the illusion of space and movement. If it leads to a bench or rock, it creates a sense of anticipation as feet or eyes follow it through even the shortest distance. A bench, a large stump, or a sitting rock placed in an out-of-the-way, half-hidden spot along the path creates the most charm. Catching a glimpse of an imposing natural feature lures the visitor into the shade to sit and enjoy.

Stepping-stones in the woodland garden serve several functions. Visually, they lead the eye into the garden and enhance its three-dimensional aspect. During the summer, stones keep foot traffic off the ground where spring-flowering plants lie dormant. Although the foliage of spring wildflowers dies to the ground, the plants lying just below the surface are damaged by repeated foot traffic. Stones half-hidden by low-growing plants reinforce the layered character of a natural garden.

 The visual line that marks the border between the shade garden and open lawn sets a tone for the landscape. An edging with straight lines and angular bends gives an energetic, electric feeling. By contrast, a smooth arc and tangent line curves around the landscape in a soothing form. Keep the curves broad and gentle. In an absent-minded effort to be interesting, some garden borders are simply too wavy. Far from being gentle and relaxing, a "wiggly" line results in an unnatural, busy look.

 The narrow arching leaves of sedges planted along the edge of the lawn or a walk echo the lawn's texture while making a transition into the shade garden. Sedges often grow in clumps rather than in a mat. One of the most ornamental and useful is the fine-leaf variegated cultivar of Japanese sedge (*Carex morrowii* 'Variegata'). The six-to ten-inch clumps of arching grasslike leaves with white edges soften the border of the garden. Sedges grow well in moist soil. Although some, like yellow nut-sedge, invade lawns with ruthless results, many are fantastic shade-garden plants. The dark green leaves of *C. jamesii,* the pale gray of *C. glauca,* and the fine-textured wood sedge *(C. laxiflora)* are other choices available in this underused group of shade plants.

 Two species, both called forget-me-not—*Brunnera macrophylla* and *Myosotis sylvatica*—add small blue flowers to the spring garden. *Brunnera's* heart-shaped foliage contrasts with the narrow leaves of *Myosotis. Myosotis* grows as a biennial and spreads easily by seed. Both grow best in moist soil rich in organic matter. The combination of bleeding heart *(Dicentra spectabilis)* and forget-me-not gives an outstanding pink-and-blue effect. In spring, when forget-me-not is topped with masses of tiny sky-blue flowers, the plant is one of the best for the edge of a shade garden. The rounded heart-shaped leaves of brunnera give a smooth leaf line along a path. When seen at a distance in a border next to the lawn, the coarse-textured foliage gives a uniform, mass effect.

At the edge of a raised bed or on a shallow slope, lamb's ears is striking. Although its scrawny flower stalks and tiny pink and lavender flowers appeal to some, they need to be cut off as they fade. Blend lamb's ears with burgundy cultivars of coralbell (*Heuchera micrantha* 'Palace Purple'), snowdrop anemone *(Anemone sylvestris),* and myrtle *(Vinca minor).* Plant near shrubs that also take reduced light, such as tree peony, summersweet *(Clethra alnifolia),* or *Daphne* x *burkwoodii.*

Small Shady Gardens

 In a small shady garden, a small tree such as a redbud, fringe tree, or Carolina silverbell, or a large shrub such as a common witch hazel, any of various viburnums, or Juneberry, produces a natural yet eye-catching effect. One of these placed alone at a corner or in any spot where it creates a focal point becomes a "specimen" plant. Use that plant as the basis on which to build the rest of the garden. Devote a space that is at least three feet wide along a fence or wall to the specimen, and add groups of herbaceous plants. If the area is longer than 20 feet, add smaller shrubs such as dwarf fothergilla or oakleaf hydrangea to create a layering effect.

In a small wildflower garden, strike a balance between plants that go dormant after flowering (the "ephemerals"), and those that keep their leaves all season ("persistent" plants). To the spring ephemerals like bloodroot *(Sanguinaria canadensis),* squirrel corn *(Dicentra canadensis),* Dutchman's-breeches *(D. cucullaria),* trillium (*Trillium* spp.), and dwarf larkspur *(Delphinium tricorne),* add delicate, slow-growing persistents such as jack-in-the-pulpit (*Arisaema* spp.), columbine *(Aquilegia canadensis),* and wild bleeding heart *(Dicentra eximia).* They attract attention yet will not overrun the area. Other persistent, delicate native wildflowers include bellwort *(Uvularia grandiflora),* blue woodland phlox *(Phlox divaricata),* Jacob's ladder *(Polemonium reptans),* and rue anemone *(Anemonella thalictroides).*

A small shade garden offers an opportunity to create an intricate blending of plants. A wall provides a planting surface for vines such as Virginia creeper, Baltic ivy, or porcelain vine (*Ampelopsis* spp.). A vine softens the hard surface and gives the illusion of a woodland scene. Although few vines bloom in the shade, many have an interesting leaf form and excellent fall color. Pick a vine that complements the space. In very small spaces, use vines with a fine texture, such as *Ampelopsis,* silver lace vine *(Polygonum*

aubertii), or a small-leaf ivy. Along a larger fence or wall use Virginia creeper, climbing hydrangea, or bigleaf wintercreeper. Since wintercreeper *(Euonymus fortunei)* and English ivy *(Hedera helix)* keep their leaves all winter, their foliage adds color to the winter garden.

 Even in the smallest garden, combine plants on three levels, or layers. Use a tall layer of trees, a second of shrubs, and a third of ground covers or herbaceous plants. This attention to vertical arrangement echoes the rhythm of natural woodlands. In a small garden, the tree layer may be a small tree or a large shrub. The difference between a small multistem tree and a large shrub is far from clear. Generally it depends only on how many main stems the plant has. If there are too many to count, consider the plant a shrub.

 Plants such as Juneberry (*Amelanchier* spp.) may be grown either as a tree or as a shrub. Flowering dogwood *(Cornus florida),* Cornelian cherry dogwood *(C. mas),* redbud *(Cercis canadensis),* American plum *(Prunus americana),* Japanese tree lilac *(Syringa reticulata),* sourgum *(Nyssa* spp.) and pawpaw *(Asimina triloba)* fit into the category of small tree. Nannyberry *(Viburnum lentago),* common witch hazel *(Hamamelis virginiana),* and American hazelnut *(Corylus americana)* are large shrubs of natural woodlands. In a small space, one of these plants strategically placed becomes a focal point. Choose one that fits the site and blends with the rest of the landscape.

For small, lightly shaded gardens, pagoda dogwood *(Cornus alternifolia)* **grows with a beautiful layered look.** It requires moist yet well-drained, slightly acid soil. A soil containing organic matter mimics the undisturbed woodland soil of its native habitat. The leaves' gentle curving veins and smooth margins, typical of all dogwoods, add to the tree's aristocratic form. Pair this elegant dogwood with herbaceous plants that complement its smooth form. Some attractive understory choices include ladyfern *(Athyrium filix-femina), Lamium maculatum* 'White Nancy', sweet woodruff *(Galium odoratum),* Allegheny spurge *(Pachysandra procumbens),* barrenwort *(Epimedium* spp.), three-colored bugleweed *(Ajuga reptans* 'Rainbow' or 'Burgundy Glow'), *Astilbe* 'Sprite', rue anemone *(Anemonella thalictroides),* and false rue anemone *(Isopyrum biternatum).*

Visual Accents for the Shade Garden

A shady rock garden highlights the plants and treats the stones as sculpture. With deliberate casualness, the half-buried boulders seem to rise from the earth like miniature cliffs in some wild place. Crown the garden with a small, interestingly shaped tree such as crab apple, hawthorn, striped maple *(Acer pensylvanicum),* or Tartarian maple *(A. tartaricum).* Planted off center, the small tree establishes an informal, natural framework for the rest of the garden. Underneath the taller plants, add a group of summersweet *(Clethra alnifolia),* fothergilla *(Fothergilla gardenii),* or low-growing cotoneaster *(Cotoneaster* spp.). Fill in the design with hellebore, pachysandra, European ginger, pulmonaria, and bergenia.

Carefully place ornamental sculpture in the garden. Popular pieces range from shiny reflecting balls to weathered stone and bronze statuary. Over time, even the most interesting piece placed out in the open blends into the background or begins to look static. Eventually, like a mailbox or a crack in the front walk, it fades from view. Placed partially hidden next to a bush or some wildflowers, the sculpture takes on the organic qualities of the garden itself. As the flowers change and the leaves fall, the personality of the sculpture evolves.

 Artificial lighting accents a woodland garden. Lights strategically placed in trees create a pattern of shadows as they shine through the branches. While the light enables visitors to enter the house and garden safely, the shadows create form and line. At night, trees lit from below or at an angle reveal an entirely new view of themselves and the garden.

 Carefully placed birdhouses add character to the garden. Although some are strictly functional, others are as eye-catching as the most brightly arrayed tropical flower. As decorative houses hang inside the canopy of the tree, they are revealed by glimpses through the leaves and produce ideal garden sculpture.

 Use fallen trunks or large branches as natural accents in the shade garden. Recently, the popularity of bronze and concrete ornaments has soared. Natural materials like wood and stone are forgotten, or if they are used, they are often carved into some contrived shape or figure. A carefully placed log turns the garden into a natural landscape, serving as a natural backdrop for low-growing herbaceous plants. A deliberate artistic eye arranges natural elements so they don't look like a pile of brush or clutter.

 A well-placed stone helps the garden look like natural woodland. When a glimpse of stone shows through greenery, hardscape or permanent features play against plant life, and the garden takes on a new dimension. To look like a natural outcropping, the stone may be partially buried. For smaller stones, allowing evergreen ground covers such as wintercreeper *(Euonymus fortunei)* to grow over them produces a similar effect.

Color in the Shade

 The burgundy-green fronds of Japanese painted fern (*Athyrium nipponicum* 'Pictum') appear lightly brushed with silver paint, creating subtle color. Its low-growing clumps work well with many other ferns and short shade-garden plants. One particularly effective combination pairs it with burgundy-flowered impatiens. The echo of the same shade seems to intensify the color. Other interesting combinations match Japanese painted fern with lungwort (*Pulmonaria* 'Sissinghurst'),

Hosta 'McDougal', and low-growing variegated sedges.

Attractive foliage plants with colors similar to Japanese painted fern are alumroot—*Heuchera micrantha* and *H. americana*. *Heuchera micrantha* 'Palace Purple' is an outstanding shade plant. Seed-grown plants are variable in color and hardiness. While the burgundy-tinted green *Heuchera americana* is very hardy, the novel white and green *Heuchera micrantha* 'Ice Palace' is not hardy north of zone six. During the heat and drought of midsummer, the purple cultivars that are planted in light shade turn a brassy, nearly orange color.

Take advantage of the many stunning colors of hosta foliage. Shades of yellow, gold, blue, and green echo and highlight the colors of the summer garden. Although there are hundreds of hosta cultivars, many are hard to find and some are very expensive. Several outstanding older cultivars have stood the test of time. In June, a brilliant combination is *Hosta plantaginea* 'Gold Standard', lady's mantle *(Alchemilla mollis),* and *Geranium grandiflorum* 'Johnson's Blue', backed by the tall, pale green ostrich fern.

The continuous blooms of annuals like impatiens and begonia bring season-long color to many shade gardens. Although time stands still for annuals, the week or two for which most perennials flower track the garden's changes from spring to fall. Finding a long-blooming shade perennial is a challenge, but a few plants, such as yellow corydalis *(Corydalis lutea),* yellow celandine poppy *(Stylophorum diphyllum),* delicate pink *Dicentra eximia* 'Luxuriant', and lavender toadflax *(Linaria purpurea),* stand out.

 Impatiens is hard to beat for brilliant, uniform summer color from the last frost in the spring until the first frost of the autumn. But the bright color that radiates in cool shade wilts in hot, dry spots. Even as the last rays of the early evening sun beam through the shadows, any impatiens caught in its glare turns limp. As the sun fades, the plants perk up. Keep them well watered and put them in the coolest, shadiest spots.

 The most natural summer garden blends flowering plants of various heights and colors in sweeps and patches throughout the shade. The one- to three-foot-tall spiderwort *(Tradescantia virginiana)* is somewhat floppy but colorful and long blooming.

Martagon lily *(Lilium martagon)* grows on flower stalks that hold over a dozen small purple to pink flowers shaped like tiny turbans. Other shade-tolerant lilies include wood lily *(Lilium philadelphicum)*, whose bright orange-red flowers show up easily through the shade, and Turk's cap lily *(Lilium superbum)*, whose flowers grow with long, dark orange sepals that curve backward and are spotted with purple.

The soft gray foliage of lamb's ears *(Stachys byzantina)* lightens dark areas near the edge of the shade garden. The pale gray cast on the fronds of Japanese painted fern serves the same purpose in deeper shade. Although most plants with gray leaves require strong light, these two grow in lower light, and along with variegated plants serve to brighten the shadows of the shady spots. For lamb's ears, light shade lessens the heat that promotes a midsummer dieback. Plant it in well-drained soil to curb the rot to which it is prone.

***Lamium maculatum,* a species from the group called—strangely enough—dead nettle, is a colorful ground cover for shade.** Although other members of the genus tend to be weedy, the *Lamium maculatum* 'White Nancy' is a good choice, with variegated green-and-white leaves and, in the spring, small sweet-pealike flowers. Perhaps as a connection to its weedy relatives, *Lamium maculatum* grows in both moist, rich soil and in drier, less fertile places. Lamium complements the broad leaves of hosta as well as the tall lacy fronds of ostrich and ladyfern. One striking and easy-to-grow combination adds the dark green, coarser texture of English ivy.

 The narrow, grasslike leaves of lilyturf *(Liriope muscari)* arch gracefully along walls and borders. Variegated lilyturf adds a tracing of white or yellow to the thin green blades. Use the yellow forms to heighten the effect of flowering plants such as yellow loosestrife *(Lysimachia punctata),* lady's mantle *(Alchemilla mollis),* or yellow corydalis *(Corydalis lutea).* The heat-tolerant lilyturf is popular in southern gardens. Although recommended for gardens in zones six to nine, in protected spots it grows as far north as Chicago. Once established, it is fairly hardy in zone five. The trick is to protect it with evergreen branches in winter.

***Corydalis lutea*'s small yellow flowers crown its lacy, yellow-green leaves.** Its six- to eight-inch mounds brighten not just rock gardens but any lightly shaded spot. The taller and more shade-tolerant celandine poppy *(Stylophorum diphyllum)* brightens the deepest shade with clear, buttercup-shaped blooms. Another long-blooming shade plant, fringed bleeding heart (*Dicentra eximia* 'Luxuriant'), exhibits the same fine-textured foliage, with flowers that dangle from stems like small pale pink lanterns. Compared to shade blooming annuals, these delicate, fine plants add quiet color to the garden.

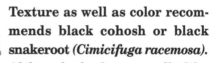

Texture as well as color recommends black cohosh or black snakeroot *(Cimicifuga racemosa).* Although the long, candle-like flower stalks can reach nearly eight feet, its large, heavily dissected and irregularly toothed leaves form attractive three-foot stands of foliage. Its leaves become an interesting backdrop for plants with contrasting foliage, such as hosta, phlox, and tradescantia. Although cultivars of garden phlox *(Phlox paniculata)* grow best in gardens in full sun and good air circulation, pale lavender phlox often invades lightly shaded gardens—to the joy of many gardeners and the dismay of others.

Trees, Shrubs, and Vines for the Shade Garden

∿ ∿

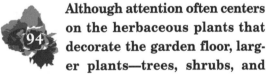 **Although attention often centers on the herbaceous plants that decorate the garden floor, larger plants—trees, shrubs, and vines—create the garden's framework and anchor it visually.** Tall trees like oaks, maples, ashes, lindens, and honey locusts create a canopy layer. Planted under and near the larger trees, smaller trees and tall shrubs like dogwood, Juneberry, American plum, blue beech, and redbud bring the woodland into human scale. Densely leaved vines carry visually across an open space to create a lush effect from the back of the gar-

den. Various species of viburnum, hydrangea, witch hazel, bottlebrush buckeye, hazelnut, leatherwood, and spicebush complete the composition.

 Trees, shrubs, and vines are an invaluable source of color, form, and texture, especially in the shade. Vivid foliage and stems and bright berries add fall and winter interest to the colorful blooms of spring and summer. Rough and smooth bark, intricate or spare patterns of branches, thick or slender stems enliven the winter landscape. A careful choice of woody plants extends the garden's beauty and helps to compensate for the subtler, less showy blooms of woodland flowers.

 A convenient rule of thumb recommends that two-thirds of the woody plants in a garden have foliage that is medium to coarse in texture. Large-leaved redbud and pawpaw form a strong backdrop for the delicate evergreen foliage of hemlock and yew. Clusters of coarser-leaved woody plants such as viburnum, rhododendron, hydrangea, and dogwood anchor fine-textured shrubs such as barberry, summersweet, and cotoneaster. Delicate flowers and foliage of woodland perennials stand out against coarse-leaved vines like Boston ivy and Virginia creeper.

Trees in the Shady Garden

Some trees are more compatible with a shade garden than others. Often trees that produce heavy shade have dense, shallow roots that crowd out the roots of other plants and deprive them of water. Large maples, beeches, and sycamores are particularly difficult to grow plants under. Spring-flowering bulbs and shallow-rooted ground covers are the best plants for these gardens.

Large old trees that discourage underplanting sometimes compensate with plants that grow directly on their surface. In temperate climates, big trees serve as habitat for many small, colorful ferns, lichens, and mosses. In subtropical gardens, epiphytic plants such as bromeliads and orchids grow in the trees.

"Limbing up" low-growing branches alters the effect of large trees in the landscape. Although pruning low-growing branches allows more light to reach the shade garden, the tree loses some of its character. Low, horizontal limbs bring the canopy of the shade garden to eye level. The natural look of large branches stretching out and bending to the ground gives the shade garden a human scale. Tulip tree *(Liriodendron tulipifera),* yellowwood *(Cladrastis lutea),* Kentucky coffee tree *(Gymnocladus dioica),* katsura tree *(Cercidiphyllum japonicum),* and Amur cork tree *(Phellodendron amurense)* form attractive low-branching patterns.

 Although crab apple (*Malus* spp.) and hawthorn (*Crataegus* spp.) often form interesting branching patterns, the small twigs inside the canopy detract from their grace and form, making them look simply bushy. When these small vertical twigs, called water sprouts, grow along the main branches, prune them. Careful pruning reveals the shape and the line of the trunk as it rises from the ground. The goal is a simple, aesthetic, and natural shape.

Shrubs and Small Trees for the Shade Garden

 The graceful, arching Japanese maple provides elegant form, texture, and color under the shade of taller trees and buildings in any garden. Even in the shade, many of the cultivars suffer at least some dieback in the harsh winters of the north. Although they do not grow as vigorously or as large in northern gardens, they are still worthwhile. Place them in sheltered spots out of winter sun and wind in well-drained, rich, slightly acid soil. Some of the more cold tolerant are the cultivar *Acer palmatum dissectum* 'Garnet' and cultivars of the related species, *Acer japonicum*.

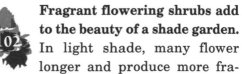

Fragrant flowering shrubs add to the beauty of a shade garden. In light shade, many flower longer and produce more fragrance than they do in full sun. Although the most fragrant spring-flowering shrub, mock orange *(Philadelphus coronarius),* grows with some afternoon shade, in dense shade it flowers less. Other fragrant spring shrubs include Korean spice viburnum *(Viburnum carlesii)* and *Daphne* spp. For midsummer fragrance, use summersweet *(Clethra alnifolia)* and Carolina allspice (*Calycanthus* spp.). Although not as fragrant as the famous Australian eucalyptus, the leaves of spicebush *(Lindera benzoin)* emit a faint scent of citrus all season.

Hydrangeas can be excellent plants for shady gardens. One popular cultivar of smooth hydrangea, *H. arborescens* 'Annabelle', is particularly showy. Although 'Annabelle' produces very large balls of greenish-white flowers nearly a foot across, in dense shade the flowers flop over and lie on the ground—not a very attractive sight. The flatter, creamier heads of the straight species *(H. arborescens)* produce a more natural look for the edge of a woodland garden.

Distinctive coarse-textured stems and oak-shaped leaves make oakleaf hydrangea (*H. quercifolia*) an unusual and attractive plant. The large-petaled, elongated panicles, or flower clusters, produced in late summer, turn an attractive bronzed-red in the fall, and the stems show exfoliating orange-tinged bark in the winter. Although it can die back to the ground during very cold winters when the temperature dips below −10 to −15°F, it does grow back and is hardy through zone five. Since it flowers on old wood, plant it in sheltered spots in colder regions.

Both native and Asian species of witch hazel (*Hamamelis* spp.) grow in shade as well as sun. Although all the witch hazels produce tiny, threadlike petals that are lightly pungent, they vary in time of bloom, color, size, hardiness, and vigor in the shady spots. The more cold-hardy common witch hazel *(H. virginiana),* grows with a large, rangy habit to roughly 20 feet. Yellow, fragrant flowers in mid autumn enhance its attractive yellow fall leaves. Vernal witch hazel *(H. vernalis)* flowers in late winter in a wide range of soil types. Although Chinese and Japanese witch hazels and the hybrid *Hamamelis* x *intermedia* are smaller and showier than the native species, they are not as hardy.

 At first glance, Japanese kerria *(Kerria japonica)* is a scruffy, tangled, anemic bush. Its buttercup-like yellow flowers along chartreuse stems and its thin, pale green leaves appear weedy and without distinction. But in winter, its thin stems remain colorfully green. In mild climates it forms a thick mass that may reach six to nine feet. Winter dieback in zones four and five requires spring pruning and results in plants that maintain their height at three to four feet.

 Although native to woodlands throughout the eastern United States, leatherwood *(Dirca palustris)* remains underused. In areas of wet shade near riverbanks and streams, leatherwood is spectacular in spring and fall. Its tiny yellow bell-like flowers appear before the leaves emerge. Its uniform gray bark and smooth-edged leaves present a graceful appearance during the summer. In fall it turns a clear yellow. Oval in shape, it grows slowly in the shade to about four feet. Since new home construction in sunny open sites supplies the largest market for plants, leatherwood doesn't always make it into the garden-center trade. It is worth looking for.

 Two good native shrubs for shade are *Fothergilla gardenii* and the larger *F. major.* They produce small white fragrant tufts of thin-petaled flowers in mid spring. With bright red and yellow leaves forming a brilliant mosaic with a few green tinges, their fall color is exquisite. During the summer, fothergilla's medium-green foliage resembles that of a close relative, witch hazel. In winter, its thin dark stems form neat, definitely articulated lines in the landscape. These slow-growing plants rarely need pruning. Since they grow best in sandy, acid swamps, finding just the right spot for them can be tricky.

 American hazelnut *(Corylus americana)* grows as an eight- to 15-foot shrub without a central leader. Since it grows by suckering from the base, it easily spreads to form a thick screen. In early spring before the leaves emerge, the male flowers form showy two- to three-inch catkins. The fall color varies from a muted yellow to red. American hazelnut is a good choice for natural areas. For better or worse in the garden, deer and rabbits feed off the American hazelnut as well as witch hazel, fothergilla, and summersweet.

 When black walnut trees form the canopy of the shade garden, the toxins in their roots inhibit the growth of many other plants. Finding plants that tolerate the shade as well as the chemicals released into the soil is a challenge. Porcelain vine (*Ampelopsis* spp.) and members of the *Hydrangea* genus will grow near walnuts. Climbing hydrangea (*Hydrangea petiolaris*) growing up the trunk of a stately mature walnut tree is an attractive sight in early summer. Other hydrangeas for similar conditions include *H. arborescens, H. quercifolia,* and *H. paniculata.*

 Although conifers produce dense shade for screening and contrast year-round, few plants, including evergreen shrubs, grow well under them. Those that do include yew (*Taxus* spp.), hemlock (*Tsuga canadensis*), false cypress (*Chamaecyparis* spp.), and fir (*Abies* spp.). Yews have short, flat, very dark green needles. Most require lots of space and will grow into trees if left unsheared. Hemlocks have a soft, fine-textured, often weeping appearance. They need well-drained, acid soil, making them a little more difficult to place. Some forms of false cypress droop gracefully in mounds of emerald and yellow-green. All of these needle-leaf evergreens screen year-round, and are ideal for creating privacy in the smaller shade garden.

Vines for the Shade

 Vines that grow with tiny twisting tendrils may damage building surfaces. Some, like English ivy *(Hedera helix)* and Boston ivy *(Parthenocissus tricuspidata),* have disklike tendril tips that stick to bricks and mortar with nearly gluelike force. Other tendril vines in the grape family are porcelain vine *(Ampelopsis)* and Virginia creeper *(Parthenocissus quinquefolia).* When grown on trees, tendril vines produce no ill effects. Twining vines like wild grape, bittersweet, and native wisteria are destructive to trees, slowly strangling them.

 Bigleaf wintercreeper (*Euonymus fortunei* 'Vegeta') is an excellent woody vine, ground cover, or shrub for shade. The slow-growing stems adapt easily to any form of growth. Short rootlike holdfasts cling to surfaces like tree trunks or walls. Although thick woody stems and leathery leaves make bigleaf wintercreeper too heavy to grow more than a few feet along a wall without support, in trees it easily climbs 20 feet. With glossy evergreen leaves and orange berries, the plant is particularly attractive in the fall and winter.

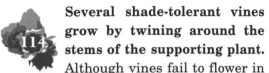 **Several shade-tolerant vines grow by twining around the stems of the supporting plant.** Although vines fail to flower in heavy shade, they are vigorous enough to spread from sun into a shaded area. Robust twining vines like bittersweet may throttle and kill the plant on which they climb. Long wires or rods formed into a tall trellis create an ideal surface for twining vines. Shade-tolerant ornamental twining vines include silver lace vine *(Polygonum aubertii),* five-leaf akebia *(Akebia quinata),* Dutchman's pipe *(Aristolochia macrophylla),* honeysuckle vine *(Lonicera* spp.), moonseed *(Menispermum canadense),* and greenbriar *(Smilax rotundifolia).* Also consider the hardy kiwis, in particular *Actinidia kolomikta.*

Berries, Fruits, and Birds

Birds are attracted to plants with small brightly colored or succulent berries. Sumac, elderberry, serviceberry or Juneberry, mulberry, chokecherry, crab apple, hawthorn, dogwood, spicebush, bayberry, winterberry, American plum, juniper, and viburnum woven together with vines and ground covers provide shelter and food. Evergreens like pine, fir, spruce, hemlock, and *Arborvitae* add cover and protection as well as seeds.

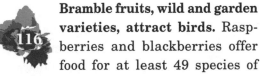

Bramble fruits, wild and garden varieties, attract birds. Raspberries and blackberries offer food for at least 49 species of birds. An unpruned area of brambles becomes a tangle of stems and thorns that provides protective cover as well. In abandoned fields, wild tangled masses attract orioles, blue jays, and gray catbirds. Although the most desirable cultivars of these fruits need full sun and plenty of moisture, wild raspberries and blackberries grow at the woodland edge.

Native elderberry (*Sambucus* spp.) volunteers in many shade gardens. In fairly dense shade, it flowers with flat clusters of creamy white in late spring. The blossoms become deep burgundy berries in fall, attracting Baltimore orioles, American robins, cardinals, blue jays, cedar waxwings, and brown thrashers, as well as people who like elderberry jam and wine. Plants form spreading colonies that reach eight to 12 feet in height. A stand of elderberry grows from one or two plants to a formidable thicket that readily spreads over 20 feet. Elderberry thrives in all sorts of soils. Although finding a local source is a challenge, many gardeners use mail-order sources that specialize in plants developed for high productivity.

Many vines and ground covers attract birds to the shade garden. Bittersweet (*Celastrus* spp.), Virginia creeper (*Parthenocissus* spp.), trumpet vine *(Campsis radicans),* and trumpet honeysuckle *(Lonicera sempervirens)* offer birds food from summer to autumn. Low-growing cotoneasters and junipers provide berries that are less succulent but last longer into the fall and winter. Hawthorn berries also hang on into the winter, giving fruit for the late winter and early spring.

A Weed Is
a Flower
Out of Place

One gardener's out-of-control weed is another's favorite flowering plant. In light shade, ladybell *(Campanula rapunculoides)* may outgrow most of its neighbors, creating a monoculture of tall, blue-flowered plants. But for gardeners seeking an easy-to-grow, attractive flower, ladybell is the end of the rainbow. Like all plants that grow in light shade, as the shade becomes deeper the plants get leggier. The bell-shaped flowers arranged along a spike typically fall over onto other plants. But for those who enjoy the tiny blue bells, its floppy form and aggressive habit come with the plant.

 Creeping Charlie *(Glechoma hederacea)* overruns many shady gardens. As its stems grow along the ground, new roots emerge from the base of every leaf stem, or petiole. Anchored by the fine network of roots, creeping Charlie overwhelms most other ground covers and woodland plants. Since creeping Charlie grows vigorously in quite cool temperatures, as soon as the snow melts it greens up and begins its annual push across the landscape. Although yanking up the long runners of growth slows it down, any broken piece left in the ground regenerates to grow again. The best nonchemical method of control is to pull the blankets of creeping Charlie early every spring.

 Although many broadleaf weeds, including creeping Charlie, can be controlled with herbicides, be sure that the product you buy lists the weed you want to control. Using an herbicide on an unlisted plant is in violation of federal law. Although few inspectors are looking over the back fence, the regulations are for the benefit of the environment as well as to ensure the effectiveness of the poison.

Spot-treating with a post-emergent broadleaf herbicide kills weeds that have already germinated. Several combinations of 2,4-D, mecoprop or MCPP, and dicamba are available. Avoid spraying in extremely hot or windy weather. Spraying a newly established lawn injures the new plants. Repeated applications of herbicide containing dicamba may harm tree roots and result in stunted tree growth. Since weeds like creeping Charlie store carbohydrates in their roots in the fall, September spraying gives the most effective control by wiping out the next season's food reserves.

 Several preemergent herbicides, including Preen, work by killing weed seeds before they sprout. When an area is infested with garlic mustard, pokeweed, lamb's quarters, or wood avens, consider localized applications of preemergents. Apply the herbicide about two weeks prior to the seeds' normal germination date, in early to mid spring. Since many desirable plants spread by seed, use preemergents carefully. In areas where sweeps of violets, columbine, and *Myosotis* spread by seed, preemergents keep new seedlings from growing.

Wild violets are the ideal woodland plant and the most obnoxious woodland weed. The tiny, pansy-shaped flowers come in every shade of blue, violet, yellow, spotted, and white. In spring they create a colorful blanket, but those with thick stems or rhizomes that grow just below the surface push out other plants and resist control. Violets with thin stems and delicate fibrous roots fit more easily into a mixed shade garden.

 Thick-rooted violets present a problem for homeowners. Over-the-counter herbicides do not kill them. Roundup, a popular nonselective herbicide, only puts tiny brown holes in the leaves. Although time-consuming, the simplest way to control wild violets is to pull them out one at a time. The chemical triclopyr does work, but it must be applied by someone with a commercial pesticide applicator's license.

 Keeping a healthy, balanced garden requires vigilance year-round. When the weather permits and you see weeds, pull them even in January and February. When trees are leafless, look for signs of insects and disease. Prune out problems such as black knot of plum or tent caterpillars. Mulching with organic compost in July helps plants conserve water and manage water stress during the hottest part of the year. A plant that is not under stress is less susceptible to insects and disease.

 The delightfully fragrant spring-flowering lily-of-the-valley *(Convallaria majalis)* and sweet woodruff *(Galium odoratum)* grow vigorously enough to create an insidious weed problem. Lily-of-the-valley pushes out into surrounding plants with underground stems or rhizomes. Sweet woodruff spreads with a shallow, fibrous root system. Hoeing or pulling sweet woodruff is easier than digging out lily-of-the valley. No herbicide selectively kills either of these plants. Sweet woodruff can be killed by broadleaf herbicides, but lily-of-the-valley, a relative of grass, cannot.

 Although the old-fashioned orange daylily *(Hemerocallis fulva)* grows in light shade, it is very fast growing and weedy. Neither the double nor the single orange daylily is as attractive as the new, less aggressive varieties whose reds and pinks are improved by some afternoon shade. Since heavy shade results in few or no flowers, other plants can be used there with more success.

At first glance, the tiny white flower clusters of garlic mustard *(Alliaria petiolata)* seem a welcome addition to the spontaneous wildflower collection. Beware of this insidious shade-garden weed. Each June and July its long thin pods erupt, sending thousands and thousands of seeds into the soil. Generally only a fraction of a plant's seeds germinate, but each garlic mustard seed sprouts and grows even in the most crowded conditions. When given enough space, the plants grow into bushy one-to three-foot plants. But when crowded, they flower and produce seed on plants that are less than an inch tall. Only the most energetic gardener can remove all of them. Although broadleaf and wide-spectrum herbicides kill them, damage to other plants may also occur.

 With the best intentions, rows of nonnative buckthorn (*Rhamnus* spp.) and honeysuckle *(Lonicera maackii* and *L. tatarica)* have been planted to form quick-growing screens between new homesites in suburban developments. In many areas, the rich diversity and color of native woodlands has been lost to these aggressive large shrubs or small trees. To remove buckthorn and honeysuckle, cut the plants flush to the ground and either paint the stumps with an appropriate herbicide or cover them with black plastic and a layer of wood chips.

Virtually all woodlands suffer from the disturbances people bring to the landscape. Left alone, a shade garden results in a monoculture of aggressive, weedy native and nonnative plants, and the rich blend of textures, forms, colors, and scents of a true climax community is impossible to attain. Watch for the weeds of woody native plants like cherry, honey locust, maple, and mulberry. Managing the woodland while the weeds are small saves time and chemicals.

 Native plants that appear in disturbed woodlands and invade shade gardens include the beautiful fall vine and most irritating and invasive weed, poison ivy (*Rhus radicans*). Although the plant is variable in appearance, recognize its distinctive three-leaflet leaf. Poison oak (*Rhus toxicodendron*) looks similar but has a smaller, more indented leaf—vaguely like fragrant sumac, in the same genus. Although poison ivy grows erect or as a vine, poison oak always grows erect, often as a bush.

Contact with either poison oak or poison ivy usually results in a rash, sometimes severe. Although washing with hot, soapy water immediately after contact may lessen the reaction, some find that rubbing the affected area with juice from jewelweed *(Impatiens pallida)* helps. To get rid of poison ivy or oak, spray plants in mid- to late summer with brush-killing herbicides that list them on the label. A vigorous plant may take repeated spraying to kill. Pulling it is not only risky, but the plant often comes back from its roots.

 The common wood sorrels *Oxalis europaea* and *O. stricta* quickly become rampant, though many of their close relatives are desirable. *Oxalis violacea* is a nonweedy, beautiful native prairie plant, and shamrock, although rarely listed as a garden plant and not winter-hardy in northern gardens, is sold as a houseplant. Black nightshade *(Solanum nigrum)*, a European invader, has an American counterpart, *Solanum americanum,* that is virtually indistinguishable to most gardeners. This more-or-less poisonous species spreads easily in fertile, shady soils.

 Plants that produce hundreds of seeds easily become invasive. Among the numerous species of bedstraw *(Galium* spp.) only sweet woodruff *(Galium odoratum)* is welcome in the garden. Although some gardens become overrun with sweet woodruff, the larger and more aggressive bedstraws always rank as weeds. Their long, sticky stems grow over other plants like a blanket. At first their light, airy appearance seems innocent. In a year or two, pulling these fast-growing plants off their neighbors becomes a ritual.

 A single pokeweed *(Phytolacca americana)* **is rather attractive.** With large oval leaves and smooth reddish stems, pokeweed grows from a single stalk up to 10 feet tall. Its attractive dangling clusters of purple berries, mature leaves, and stems are very poisonous to eat—not to touch. Although the thick taproot is hard to pull out, the prolific seedlings pose a bigger weeding problem.

 In larger woodland gardens, burs often appear. Clothing and pets become magnets for these shady invaders. In spring, two that look harmless enough are bur marigold, or beggar ticks, and avens. Beggar ticks *(Bidens* spp.) include plants whose tiny yellow or greenish flowers turn into small, flat seeds with hooks. Avens *(Geum* spp.) grows from a basal rosette of interestingly shaped, pinnately compound leaves. Pull these weeds in the early spring as they emerge, or spot-treat them with a broadleaf herbicide.

Two natives from Japan have a secure, weedy foothold in our landscapes. Used first as ornamentals, kudzu and Japanese knotweed escaped cultivation and grow in shade and sun. Rarely flowering north of Virginia, kudzu grows over trees and abandoned buildings, creating an eerie sight for the uninitiated. Emerging shoots of Japanese knotweed *(Polygonum cuspidatum)* resemble bamboo at first, and then produce large broadly oval leaves with pointed tips. Their tiny white flower clusters held at the top of their four- to 10-foot stems stand out along the woodland edge. They survive into southern Canada.

Among tall, stately perennials, plume poppy *(Macleaya cordata)* reaches eight feet with a very interesting color and texture. The large, deeply lobed leaves look as if they have been cut out by design. The pale gray-green color is an attractive backdrop for many finer-textured plants. In a sunny area, it spreads vigorously by underground stems. In an area of some shade, as at the edge of a shade garden, it grows less vigorously and can be a good choice. It won't grow far into the shade like Japanese knotweed, and if it spreads into the lawn, it can be mowed off.

Particularly in small gardens, maintaining a balance among native wildflowers, nonnative shade plants, and weeds is critical. Invasive plants quickly overrun a small garden. A good design boils down to knowing what to leave out and what to remove. Canada wild ginger *(Asarum canadense)* spreads more quickly than European ginger *(A. europaeum).* Celandine poppy *(Stylophorum diphyllum),* dame's rocket *(Hesperis matronalis),* and white snakeroot *(Eupatorium rugosum)* sweep quickly through a shade garden. Some cultivars of lungwort *(Pulmonaria saccharata)* spread vigorously. The cultivar 'Sissinghurst White' does not. Whether they are weeds or wildflowers, pull unwanted aggressive plants.

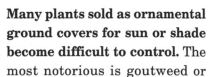 **Many plants sold as ornamental ground covers for sun or shade become difficult to control.** The most notorious is goutweed or bishop's weed *(Aegopodium podagraria).* It creeps through the landscape by underground stems or rhizomes. Once established, it is nearly impossible to remove. Variegated ribbon grass *(Phalaris arundinacea)* is equally attractive and aggressive, and also spreads by rhizomes. Planting both of them in bottomless containers such as five-gallon buckets with the bottoms cut out usually keeps them from spreading. Plants that sink

roots deeper than the buckets aren't even slowed down.

 Tall species of bamboo makes a dense screen of lush tropical beauty, but since most shade-tolerant bamboo spreads vigorously from underground stems, it quickly becomes a nuisance plant. Confine all bamboo with some kind of heavy plastic or metal underground barrier that extends at least 18 inches deep. One of the more cold-hardy species that grows in the shade is *Phyllostachys nuda*. It grows between 40 and 70 inches tall, spreads by underground rhizomes, and survives a minimum temperature of −20°F.

 Although turf grass doesn't grow well in low light, it can still be a nuisance in a shade garden. Woodland gardens grow out from the deepest shade to catch some direct or filtered light. At the border between the lawn and the garden, grass creeps into any open space, choking delicate plants like columbine (*Aquilegia* spp.) and foam flower *(Tiarella cordifolia)*. Pull sprouts of turf as they emerge. Although preemergent weedkillers applied in early spring and again in the fall help control grassy as well as broadleaf weeds, they will also kill seeds of iris, lily, Solomon's seal, and trillium.

Recreating a natural woodland requires precise planning and management, including aggressive pulling of invasive, weedy shade plants. Jumpseed or Virginia knotweed *(Tovara virginiana)*, enchanter's nightshade (*Circaea* spp.), black nightshade *(Solanum nigrum)*, garlic mustard, various kinds of avens, and ground ivy or creeping Charlie are among the weediest plants. If any one of them gains a foothold, the shade garden can be overgrown within just a few years.

Soils in
the Shade

～： ～：

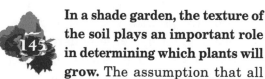

In a shade garden, the texture of the soil plays an important role in determining which plants will grow. The assumption that all dirt is equal results in a plant mortality rate of roughly 50 percent. Soil texture ranges from coarse sand to heavy clay. Sandier soil tends to drain more rapidly than clay soil. Plants that do not tolerate "wet feet" won't grow in heavy clay soil whether the site is sunny or shady. To check the texture, make a ball of moist soil. Stick a thumb into the ball. If it breaks up easily, the texture is low in clay and friable. If a huge thumbprint remains in an otherwise intact ball, the soil is mostly clay.

～：

Most woodland plants reject growing sites consisting of a few trees planted in heavy clay soil. In nature, flowers and the forest soil evolve together over hundreds of years as the annual layer of leaves decays and trees die, improving soil texture and fertility. In heavy clay, try herbaceous plants like Siberian squill, celandine poppy, common buttercup, and hosta, which grow in wide range of soils. One woody shrub for poor, shady soils is black jetbead *(Rhodotypos scandens)*.

 Attempting to amend heavy clay soil with a thick layer of compost or decayed wood chips may create new problems. Roots tend to grow into soil where there is the least resistance to their growth. A band of light growing media on top of a layer of hard soil discourages growth into the heavier clay. Create a transition layer of soil by lightly disking compost into the top inch of soil.

 Resist the temptation to spread topsoil under trees in an effort to improve soil, change the soil grade, or cover up protruding roots. In an oak woods, even a few extra inches of soil can block the natural exchange of gases from tree roots, slowly suffocating them. Although the decline may take years, eventually the fill will kill the trees. Decayed leaves, compost, or decayed wood chips do not have the same effect as a heavy blanket of fill soil.

 Even if soil texture accommodates a plant, the soil pH may not. Most plants thrive in a relatively narrow band of pH. A soil test is the best way to confirm the degree of acid or base in soil. A neutral soil has a pH of 7; acid soils have lower and basic soils have higher pHs. Although exceptions exist, most Midwest, plains, and western soils are neutral to basic, while the southeastern and eastern regions have acid soils. Soils where the bedrock is limestone are less acidic than soils resting on igneous rock and sandstone.

 Most shade garden plants thrive in slightly acid soils in a range of 6.0 to 6.5. To lower the pH for most shade-loving plants, several soil amendments are effective. A layer of composted manure helps recreate the natural organic base of most shade-garden soil. Elemental sulfur, commonly called flowers of sulfur, or ammonium and aluminum sulfate lower the pH also. Since aluminum accumulates in the soil, overuse of aluminum sulfate may lead to a toxic buildup.

Although many gardeners believe oak-leaf mulch acidifies the soil, the amount of acid in oak leaves reflects the soil and the water on which they are grown. Groundwater pumped from aquifers in limestone will be as alkaline or more alkaline than the soil. Even after the leaves dry out, residues of the chemicals that make them alkaline persist, amplifying rather than compensating for the soil's natural character.

 Mulching with pine needles helps lower pH more consistently than does mulching with oak leaves. Since the tannins and resins manufactured by conifers are acidic, pine needles gathered even in alkaline soils will be acidic. Composted pine needles make a good base for acid-loving shade plants.

 Plants shaded by a building or wall may suffer from the crushed limestone gravel used around the foundation. Limestone gravel contains chemicals that leach into the soil, raising the pH. A better strategy is to spread shredded bark or other natural material next to the foundation. In dry spots, the bark will break down very slowly while holding what moisture is present. Although decorative marble gravel is inert and will hold moisture, it does not decompose, and eventually weeds begin to grow in it. Pulling or spraying to control foundation weeds adds to the maintenance of the garden.

 In regions of the country with alkaline soils, simply adding sulfur or pine-needle mulch may not be adequate for plants requiring a pH below 6 or thereabouts. Then special planting beds must be constructed. Dig out the existing soil and replace it with equal quantities of pine mulch and peat moss. Mix this with the soil remaining in the planting area to create a transition zone. Plant in the peat moss–pine mixture. Avoid watering acid-loving plants with ground water that is alkaline. Use only rainwater that is collected in barrels and saved for the purpose.

 In well-drained acid soils with part shade, common winterberry *(Ilex verticillata)* produces an outstanding fall and winter display of red berries. Winterberry grows in soils with a pH of 4.5 to 5.5. Low-growing plants for well-drained acid soils include partridgeberry *(Mitchella repens)*, barren strawberry *(Waldsteinia fragarioides)*, trailing arbutus *(Epigaea repens)*, and bunchberry *(Cornus canadensis)*. They produce lovely spring flowers and interesting summer berries. When planted in soils that suit their requirements, foam flower (*Tiarella* spp.) and barrenwort (*Epimedium* spp.) form thick, vigorous mats. They grow slower, with some signs of chlorosis or yellowing, in higher-pH soils. For wetter acid soils, use goldthread *(Coptis groenlandica),* shield fern *(Dryopteris spinulosa),* and Canada mayflower *(Maianthemum canadense).* Wintergreen *(Gaultheria procumbens)* grows in acid soils with a wide range of moisture.

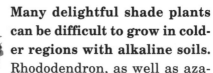

Many delightful shade plants can be difficult to grow in colder regions with alkaline soils. Rhododendron, as well as azalea, holly, pieris, leucothoe, boxwood, and sourwood, thrives in a pH as low as 4.5. In addition, these plants require well-drained soils and do best where winter temperatures remain above −10°F. If they do survive in adverse conditions, they are never very vigorous and often have yellow or chlorotic leaves.

Soil in the shade garden may be full of roots from nearby trees. When the soil is light and easy to dig, plant directly into the spaces between the larger roots. Avoid digging or rototilling the entire area. Although tree roots grow close to the surface of the soil, cutting the smaller ones won't damage the trees and shrubs that dominate the woods. Water the area well immediately after planting. Do not allow the newly planted area to dry to the point of wilting.

 Where larger roots weave a carpet under the soil, holes for shrubs or larger plants may be impossible to dig. Cutting larger roots may be inevitable. Plant shrubs and larger plants as far from the trunks of trees as possible. The farther away from the trunk, the smaller the roots. Use a sharp spade or lopping shears to avoid tearing roots. When cleanly cut, roots heal and form new side shoots.

 The ground under mature trees is often very dry. In a natural setting, leaf litter and decaying bark hold moisture for the woodland plants and the trees under which they grow. To mimic nature, spread composted bark around trees to a maximum depth of four inches. Plant shade-loving and native woodland plants in this layer of mulch mixed with soil. The mulch gives plant roots the space and moisture they need to grow.

Piling uncomposted bark chips around the base of a tree provides a breeding ground for many unwanted organisms. Although organic litter accumulates in a natural forest setting, excessive amounts may become a home and food for insects, rodents, and diseases. Mice and insects easily tunnel through thick layers of dry, undecomposed wood chips. While bacterial and fungal organisms feed on fresh wood chips, they pull nitrogen out of the surrounding soil. Pale green leaves signal nitrogen stress.

 Shredded leaves decay more quickly than leaves that are left whole. Large leaves form a mat over the ground that smothers plants as they emerge in spring. Lack of air circulation causes the leaves to decompose much more slowly than leaves cut up by a mower or a shredder. Disease-causing fungi and bacteria thrive under the soggy, airless layer. Plants often rot under the mass. By March, even shredded leaves may mat down enough to create a problem.

 As soon as the days are consistently above freezing, begin to pull leaves away from the crowns of perennials like *Primula* and *Pulmonaria*. Clean up leaves covering small spring-flowering bulbs like crocus and squill.

When low-growing spring-flowering plants remain buried, their flowering season comes and goes without notice. In northern gardens, the large semievergreen leaves of perennials such as Lenten rose and bergenia obscure new growth. Remove the previous year's foliage as new growth emerges.

 Shredded leaves decomposing in a pile is called leaf mold. The difference between leaf mold and general compost is that compost usually contains all sorts of plant parts, from grass clippings to kitchen peelings. Plant debris decomposes fastest when it is layered with a shovelful of soil and kept moist. Although leaf mold is lower in nitrogen than many other composted materials, it makes excellent mulch for insulating the soil and for improving soil texture. Fill a fenced bin or square three to six feet across and at least 18 inches high with leaves, and keep them well watered.

 Start or enlarge a shade garden by layering composted mulch under a tree. Make sure the layer of organic matter is well decayed. Mixing decayed bark into composted kitchen and garden waste mimics the natural materials found in the top layers of the forest floor. If bark is freshly shredded, the bacteria that cause it to decay will use nitrogen present in the soil to do the job. The resulting nitrogen deficiency will cause plants to appear pale green and to grow more slowly than usual.

 Trees and shrubs help compensate for moderate temperature swings. Although in mild climates plants such as sea thrift grow in open sunny sites, they grow best with part shade in southern gardens. In harsh northern climates, trees protect slow-emerging spring plants growing under their branches by delaying their growth. When plants emerge later, the buds suffer less damage from sudden cold snaps.

 Some trees and flowering plants are well suited for low-lying, wet areas. Swamp white oak *(Quercus bicolor)*, pin oak *(Q. palustris)*, bald cypress *(Taxodium distichum)*, and various alders *(Alnus* spp.) easily constitute a framework for poorly drained sites. Astilbe *(Astilbe* spp.), joe-pye weed *(Eupatorium purpureum)*, white snakeroot *(E. rugosum)*, black snakeroot *(Cimicifuga racemosa)*, cardinal flower *(Lobelia* spp.), turtlehead *(Chelone* spp.), bleeding heart *(Dicentra spectabilis)*, *Ligularia,* and goat's beard *(Aruncus* spp.) provide a tall, three- to eight-foot layer in moist soils. Shorter cultivars of astilbe *(Astilbe* 'Sprite') flower in early summer. The spring-flowering forget-me-not (*Myosotis* spp.), and heartleaf brunnera *(Brunnera macrophylla)* flower in a low, colorful mat of blue.

 A favorable site for a rock garden combines sandy soil texture with good drainage and some degree of shade. If the soil remains soggy for a day or two after a heavy rain, the site is poorly drained. Plants such as candytuft (*Iberis* spp.), corydalis (*Corydalis* spp.), Kenilworth ivy *(Cymbalaria muralis),* and campanula (*Campanula* spp.) will suffer root rot in poorly drained soil. Hard clay soil fails to meet the requirements of a shady rock garden.

 Repeated foot traffic in the woods compacts soil and damages dormant bulbs. Beauties such as Dutchman's-breeches *(Dicentra cucullaria),* bloodroot *(Sanguinaria canadensis),* and the large white *Trillium grandiflorum* grow best in rich, light, well-drained soil. From fall until they sprout in early spring, their delicate shoots lie dormant just below the surface. They are easily crushed. Mark the area where delicate spring wildflowers are planted with a small broken twig.

Planting and Transplanting in the Shade Garden

꒰ ꒱

169 In gardening circles, the statement "The right plant for the right place" is a cliché. However, knowing what makes a spot suitable for a particular plant defines the successful gardener. Choose plants that are suited to the soil, climate, drainage, and light conditions of the garden. Spend the small amount of time it takes to research the plant's growing requirements. Plants cannot be willed to survive in conditions that are fundamentally unsuitable. Although changing the soil pH, improving drainage, and amending the area with organic matter works some of the time, picking plants with the site in mind makes the best garden.

 Begin planting the shade garden at the drip line, or edge of the tree's canopy, rather than near the trunk. Since the tree's roots are thickest and shade densest close to the trunk, that is the darkest, driest spot in the woods. Start the plants where access to water and light is greater and allow them to become established there. Gradually, vigorously growing plants will spread into the drier, shadier areas.

 Late summer and early fall is the ideal time to transplant spring-flowering bulbs. These plants become dormant shortly after flowering. While they are dormant, moving them does not interfere with their natural growth cycle. After the foliage dies back and before the roots begin to grow, dig them with a trowel, spade, or garden fork. Separate the clump of bulbs and replant them. As the temperature of the soil cools, their new roots begin to grow. When it freezes, growth stops and starts again in early spring.

Spring and early summer are the best times to transplant shade plants that grow throughout the season. Hosta, hellebore, liriope, asarum, epimedium, bergenia, pachysandra, and vinca are a few that keep their foliage throughout the growing season or the entire year. These plants need plenty of time for their roots to grow before freezing temperatures halt development. In areas of the country where winters are mild, transplanting into late summer or fall is fine. The key to winter survival is simply that roots must be well established before the plants go dormant.

Some shade-loving flowers grow easily from seeds scattered onto the ground. Shake the pods or heads of spent flowers over areas where new color is wanted. Broadcast seeds of forget-me-not *(Myosotis sylvatica)* and dame's rocket *(Hesperis matronalis)* result quickly in showy early-spring displays. About this time, shades of lavender and white woodland phlox *(Phlox divaricata)* fill the woodland edges. Later in the spring and often continuing into the summer, celandine poppy *(Stylophorum diphyllum)* and yellow corydalis *(Corydalis lutea)* warm up the woods with yellow.

Native white snakeroot *(Eupatorium rugosum)* spreads quickly to transform autumn woodlands into drifts of white. This plant has played an interesting part in history. It was white snakeroot that Mrs. Lincoln's cow ate, poisoning its milk and leaving young Abraham Lincoln motherless. Although most gardeners aren't grazing cows in the woods anymore, weeding out excess seedlings remains part of gardening with vigorously spreading plants. Sun-loving members of the *Eupatorium* genus that spread by seed and bloom in late summer are hardy ageratum *(E. coelestinum)* and joe-pye weed *(E. purpureum).*

Many native woodland wildflowers spread naturally from seed. When the soil and drainage are suitable, spring-flowering anemones *(Anemonella thalictroides* and *Isopyrum biternatum),* wild geranium *(Geranium maculatum),* Solomon's seal *(Polygonatum* spp.), false Solomon's seal *(Smilacina racemosa),* dogtooth violet *(Erythronium* spp.), *Trillium* spp., squirrel corn and Dutchman's-breeches *(Dicentra* spp.), mayapple *(Podophyllum peltatum),* Jack-in-the-pulpit *(Arisaema triphyllum),* and bloodroot *(Sanguinaria canadense)* form clusters. To encourage these delicate beauties, pull other plants and weeds around them to reduce the competition. Don't let plants like hosta or weeds like garlic mustard invade their space. They need room to grow.

 Don't just pop plants into the ground. Most commercial growers use artificial media to grow plants. These artificial soils contain just peat moss, perlite, and sometimes ground-up bark, and they dry out at a different rate than natural woodland soils. Shake off some of the potting mix in which a new plant arrives and mix some natural ground soil around the roots to help them get established. Water the new garden plants immediately and monitor them daily. Small herbaceous plants can quickly dry out.

 Although narcissus will not grow in deep shade, they flourish in glades or woodland edges where sun pours in during the early spring. Since the bulbs become dormant in late spring, midsummer shade isn't a problem. They need the spring sun and bloom with their trumpets facing south. Plant them to the north or east of the area from which they will be viewed. To naturalize daffodils, gently toss handfuls of bulbs into the air and plant them where they fall. The staggered clusters look more natural than rows or tight little groups.

Plant broadleaf evergreens in a spot sheltered from winter sun and wind in rich, well-drained, acid soil. Winter shade protects broadleaf evergreens from drying out. Rhododendron, boxwood *(Buxus* spp.) Oregon holly grape *(Mahonia aquifolium),* evergreen holly *(Ilex* spp.) and bigleaf wintercreeper *(Euonymus fortunei)* easily suffer winter burn. Since the plants cannot take up water from roots frozen in the ground, the leaves wilt easily on cold, sunny, windy days. If adverse conditions persist, their leaves turn brown and drop off.

Transform areas with even a few trees to a lush shade garden. First remove the thin, ratty-looking grass and weeds like creeping Charlie that usually accompany it. Avoid weedkillers that travel into the plant systemically through the roots. Since herbicides such as Roundup are absorbed only through growing leaves, these sprays kill undergrowth without damaging the trees. Take care not to spray the foliage of desirable plants nearby. On a windy day the spray may drift. On an extremely hot day (over 95°F) the chemicals may volatilize and damage nearby plants.

To clear the planting area without chemicals, cover it with a layer of black plastic for several weeks. Although this method uses no chemicals, the roots of the tree are still affected. A blanket of plastic over a wide area blocks water, oxygen, and carbon dioxide from entering and leaving tree roots. Spread the plastic on a section at a time. Check the area under the plastic every few days. Leave it on only long enough to kill the unwanted plants.

Maintaining the Shade Garden

❧ ❧

Many floppy plants that bloom in light shade will benefit from pruning. Cushion spurge *(Euphorbia epithymoides)* has mounds of small yellow flowers in early spring. In midsummer, when the plant begins to flop over, cut it back to a few inches from the ground. White wood aster *(Aster divaricatus)* blooms with hundreds of tiny white flowers in shade. It will get very tall and fall over unless it is pruned back in early summer. Asters need to be cut to about 12 inches by late June. The resulting flowers will bloom on shorter, sturdier stems.

Fresh air, natural light, and rainwater invigorate houseplants. Keep them out of direct light and scrupulously check them for insects or diseases before bringing them back inside. Outside, beneficial insects keep destructive pests from taking hold. Inside, infected plants quickly sicken. Usually, hosing them down will knock off any pests. If necessary, quarantine infested houseplants and spray them with an appropriate pesticide before taking them indoors.

Some species of phlox grow well in the shade. One of the most reliable native plants, woodland phlox *(Phlox divaricata)* blooms with iris, violets, and columbine in the spring. Later in the summer, the tall garden phlox *(Phlox paniculata)* flowers with easy vigor in light shade. To minimize the coating of powdery mildew that afflicts phlox in late summer, avoid crowding the plants. This helps promote good air circulation and slows down the disease. Although garden phlox foliage looks very ratty covered with powdery mildew and yellow dying leaves, the plants survive, bloom, and spread throughout lightly shaded spots.

Although the yellow trumpets of daffodils herald the new growing season, their foliage soon fades and goes dormant. The sight of their slowly yellowing foliage detracts from the rest of the garden during the peak of summer. Plant them in the vicinity of bold, interesting plants such as hosta, Solomon's seal, or lily to distract the eye from their withering foliage. Encourage them to go dormant with a little compost. As their leaves turn seriously yellow, bend them over and partially cover them with a shovelful of compost.

 Periodic dividing and transplanting keeps plants blooming and enlarges the collection. When daffodils and narcissus stop blooming, it is a sign that they need transplanting—usually to a sunnier spot. Since their leaves produce carbohydrates needed for growth, the best time to dig most spring-flowering shade plants is after the foliage dies back. Fall is the traditional time to dig and transplant native spring-flowering plants such as trillium, Dutchman's-breeches, squirrel corn, mayapple, bloodroot, spring beauty, and dogtooth violet. Narcissus can be dug either in the spring or fall. It is not necessary to wait until they go dormant.

Apply lawn fertilizer in shady areas at half the rate used in sunny areas. Reducing the amount of fertilizer discourages diseases and unwanted plants. If the soil is damp and shady, moss thrives—grass doesn't. To control moss, increase the amount of light, improve general conditions for the turf, or plant other shade-loving plants as ground cover in place of grass.

 Some flowering plants must be left in the garden, not picked. Leaves produce the carbohydrates plants need to grow. If all the leaves grow on the stem with the flowers, picking them removes the plant's ability to store food. The distinctive three-petaled flower of trillium grows from a single stem. Just below the flower, three leaves mirror its form. If the stem is picked, the plant disappears, not to return the following spring.

 As new leaves sprout, remove the old semievergreen leaves of hellebore. The leaves are large and decay slowly. Although they are green into the winter, the plants flower in late winter and early spring on freshly emerged leaves. Removing the dead leaves gives the current year's plants a more ornamental and less messy look. Since hellebores grow slowly and clumps should not be divided until they are at least 12 inches across, cleanup is all the care hellebores require.

 Large, slowly decaying leaves from the previous year promote diseases in newly emerging plants. Although leaf mulch helps insulate plants during the winter, a blanket of heavy, wet leaves gives fungus, bacteria, and insects a perfect environment to grow. In areas with poorly drained soil, leaves that are not decomposed promote crown rot in many plants. When possible, shred leaves before putting them onto the garden. As new growth surfaces, pull thick layers of wet leaves away from the crowns.

 Although many seek for the perfect grass to grow in the shade, the search is misguided. Turf roots compete with tree roots. Grasses that grow in shade rarely form a dense, thick turf. The blades of shade-tolerant grasses are thin, and between each blade the soil shows through like the scalp on a balding head. When a mower or a weed-eater hits a tree—even gently—permanent damage results. The tree is destined to an early death. Use plants that don't need to be mowed or mulched under the drip line of a tree.

To maintain vigorous, healthy gardens, shade plantings should be fertilized annually. Autumn is the best time to fertilize woody plants. Before the ground freezes and the plants go dormant, the roots absorb the nutrients. When the first growth begins in the spring, the nutrients are in place, ready to spur on the first flush of growth. Fall fertilization will not trick plants into trying to grow through the winter. The mechanism that controls dormancy is not regulated by nutrients but rather by the day length and temperature.

 Broadcasting a granular 10-10-10 fertilizer at the rate of one to two pounds per 1,000 square feet supplies both the trees and the plants growing under them. Make sure the application is even. A thick layer of fertilizer kills plants as quickly as dousing them with table salt. Spread the fertilizer throughout the area under the drip line. Using a bulb planter to dig a grid of small holes throughout the area is an alternate method. Fill each hole with no more than a quarter cup of fertilizer.

 Warm winter days followed by subzero nights often kill shallow-rooted plants. The rapid rise and fall in temperature heaves them out of the ground. Whenever possible, use natural materials as winter mulch to insulate the more tender, newly established, or shallow-rooted plants. Since straw and hay scatter easily over the yard, they can detract from the natural beauty of winter. Recycled Christmas tree branches make an ideal natural mulch layer for the winter garden.

 Rabbit and deer can devastate a woodland garden. Although they feed on tender growth throughout the garden, rabbits do their worst damage by biting small trees and shrubs inches from the ground. Deer browse on tree limbs and shrubs so efficiently that deer-eaten shrubs look as if trimmed by a barber. On branches too large to chew off, both deer and rabbit strip the bark. Deer relish prized herbaceous plants such as trillium and hosta. Repellents are expensive and must be reapplied regularly. Enclosing each plant with a wire fence or basket is the most effective way to protect it. Usually by midsummer, the problem subsides—to reappear during the winter foraging season.

On frigid, sunny days a brisk wind quickly dries leaf tissue. Even in the shade, broadleaf evergreens suffer in north central and plains states where dramatic spikes in temperature and strong winds occur.

Leaves may grow back, but often the flower buds have been killed. Protect rhododendron, azalea, and other broadleaf evergreens by covering them with straw or dry shredded leaves. Since winter mulch easily blows off the plants, surround them with snow fencing to hold the mulch inside.

 Watch the shade garden for signs of water stress. Tree roots compete efficiently with surrounding plants for water and nutrients. Although roots are shallower in heavy clay soil than in well-drained lighter soils, typically a majority of fine feeder roots fill only the top six inches of soil, allowing them to drain the topsoil efficiently. Although they may spread for hundreds of feet from the trunk, the majority are packed in the soil near the drip line of the tree's canopy.

 Newly planted shade ground covers flourish when they receive enough water. Enriching the soil with organic matter usually does the trick. To help the soil hold moisture, add up to three or four inches of rich organic matter to the area before planting. Garden compost, mushroom compost, well-rotted horse or cow manure, and decayed wood chips make good soil amendments. Water newly planted ground covers thoroughly after planting. Check them daily to make sure they don't dry out. The smaller the ball of roots, the more quickly they dry.

 The management of topsoil in a shade garden is a delicate balance between the needs of the trees and the needs of the forest floor. While newly planted trees and shrubs are easily killed by overwatering, newly planted herbaceous plants—especially in the shade garden—dry out quickly. Newly planted trees should never be watered more than every seven to 14 days. Newly planted small herbaceous plants may need daily watering for the first few days or weeks. Poke around with a finger or trowel to determine how wet or dry the soil is, and spot-water where needed.

 During periods of extended drought, water the established shade garden by soaking the entire area under the drip line of the tree. Calibrate the sprayer by placing tin cans or water gauges in about three places under the shower from the sprayer. Collect an average of one inch of water in the cans. An inch of water should penetrate into the average soil to a depth of roughly six inches. This is enough water to maintain the garden. Don't water again for at least one to two weeks. If any measurable rain falls, check to see how far the water has penetrated before adding more.

During a prolonged drought, watering trees is more important than watering lawns. Lawns can go dormant in the summer, but trees cannot. A brown, parched lawn in July grows back during the cool, rainy days of autumn. More than a month of rainless summer days can pass before a lawn begins to die. Trees and shrubs are more shallowly rooted than turf grass. Depending on temperature and humidity, after two to three weeks without rain in midsummer, trees and shrubs begin to suffer.

Index

⌣: ⌣:

Please note: This index gives tip numbers, not page numbers. Plants are indexed by common name unless only the scientific name is in general use.